LEARN HOW TO WRITE IN

3 IN 1
LETTERS
WORDS
SENTENCES

CURSIVE FOR KIDS

This Book Belongs To

Andrea Holden

Author Note

Thank you for purchasing this book. I would love to receive your feedback about this book by submitting a review in the Amazon marketplace from which you purchased it.

Amazon reviews are really helpful to better rank books and make them visible to more people, so that buyers can make the best choice by selecting from a larger set of offers.

Moreover, I read all submitted reviews and make sure to take your comments / critics into consideration when designing my next books. I also enjoy reading how people express their satisfaction and how my books have helped them in their daily life endeavors.

I really appreciate your contribution ☺

Andrea Holden

Printed in the United States of America

First Printing, 2020

ISBN 9798690449872

Table of contents

This Cursive Handwriting workbook is divided into the following sections:

Kids can use a pencil, light color marker or a highlighter to trace the dotted cursive letters and words.

Introduction

Cursive is a style of writing in which all the letters in a word are connected. It's also known as script or longhand. When the third-grade students learned cursive writing, they were excited to find that they could write entire words without lifting their pencil from the paper.

Cursive comes from the past participle of the Latin word 'currere', which means "to run." In cursive handwriting, the letters all run into one another and the hand runs across the page, never lifting between letters. Every time a document asks for your signature at the bottom of a document, you are meant to use this flowing cursive writing style.

When students are taught the English language in only one form, print writing, they get only one chance to learn and memorize the letters. By having to learn cursive as well, students get another opportunity to fully comprehend the alphabet. Learning cursive also gives students a clearer understanding of how letters are formed, which will improve their print writing as well.

Fascinating new research points out the benefits of cursive writing for cognitive development. One study concluded that elementary students need at least "15 minutes of handwriting daily for cognitive, writing and motor skills and reading comprehension improvement." An article in *'Psychology Today'* cited research which shows that:

- Students "*wrote more words, faster, and expressed more ideas when writing essays by hand versus with a keyboard.*" This study included second, fourth, and sixth graders.

- "*Cursive writing helps train the brain to integrate visual (and) tactile information, and fine motor dexterity.*"

- The regions of the brain that are activated during reading were "*activated during hand writing, but not during typing.*"

Unfortunately, more and more school districts across the country are forgoing the teaching of cursive writing in the classroom (presumably to give kids yet more time to practice for standardized tests). We can understand where districts are coming from — who uses cursive writing as much as they print these days? So much of writing is done by keyboard, after all. Aren't we better off teaching kids how to type properly? Yes , we should be teaching typing, too, but not in place of cursive. An art must never be left behind!

Fortunately, this Cursive Handwriting workbook is designed to close the gap and help kids of all ages to start learning to write cursive letters, words and sentences and to improve their handwriting. Kids can gain mastery over cursive writing using an easy dot-to-dot tracing method.

SECTION 1

LEARNING THE CURSIVE ALPHABET

ABC

Trace and then copy each letter of the alphabet, both lowercase and uppercase, until you master each one.

a is for
ant

Trace the lowercase letters, then write your own.

𝑎 𝑎 𝑎 𝑎 𝑎 𝑎

𝑎 𝑎

𝑎

Trace the uppercase letters, then write your own.

𝐴 𝐴 𝐴 𝐴 𝐴

𝐴 𝐴

𝐴

Trace the lowercase letter, then write your own.

Trace the uppercase letter, then write your own.

A B C D E F G H I J K L M N O P Q R S T U V W X Y Z

b is for bear

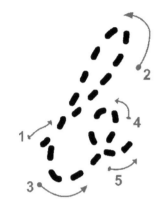

Trace the lowercase letters, then write your own.

Trace the uppercase letters, then write your own.

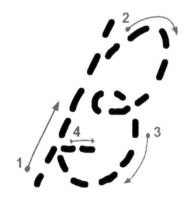

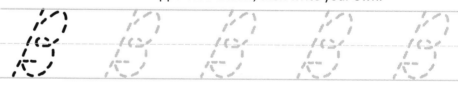

A B C D E F G H I J K L M N O P Q R S T U V W X Y Z

Trace the lowercase letter, then write your own.

Trace the uppercase letter, then write your own.

A B C D E F G H I J K L M N O P Q R S T U V W X Y Z

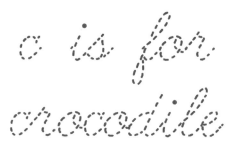

c is for crocodile

Trace the lowercase letters, then write your own.

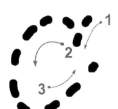

Trace the uppercase letters, then write your own.

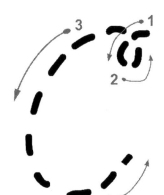

A B **C** D E F G H I J K L M N O P Q R S T U V W X Y Z

Trace the lowercase letter, then write your own.

Trace the uppercase letter, then write your own.

A B C D E F G H I J K L M N O P Q R S T U V W X Y Z

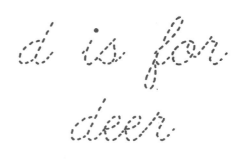

Trace the lowercase letters, then write your own.

Trace the uppercase letters, then write your own.

A B C **D** E F G H I J K L M N O P Q R S T U V W X Y Z

Trace the lowercase letter, then write your own.

Trace the uppercase letter, then write your own.

A B C **D** E F G H I J K L M N O P Q R S T U V W X Y Z

e is for elephant

Trace the lowercase letters, then write your own.

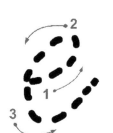

Trace the uppercase letters, then write your own.

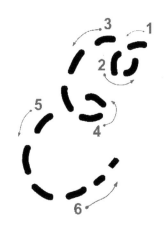

A B C D **E** F G H I J K L M N O P Q R S T U V W X Y Z

Trace the lowercase letter, then write your own.

Trace the uppercase letter, then write your own.

A B C D **E** F G H I J K L M N O P Q R S T U V W X Y Z

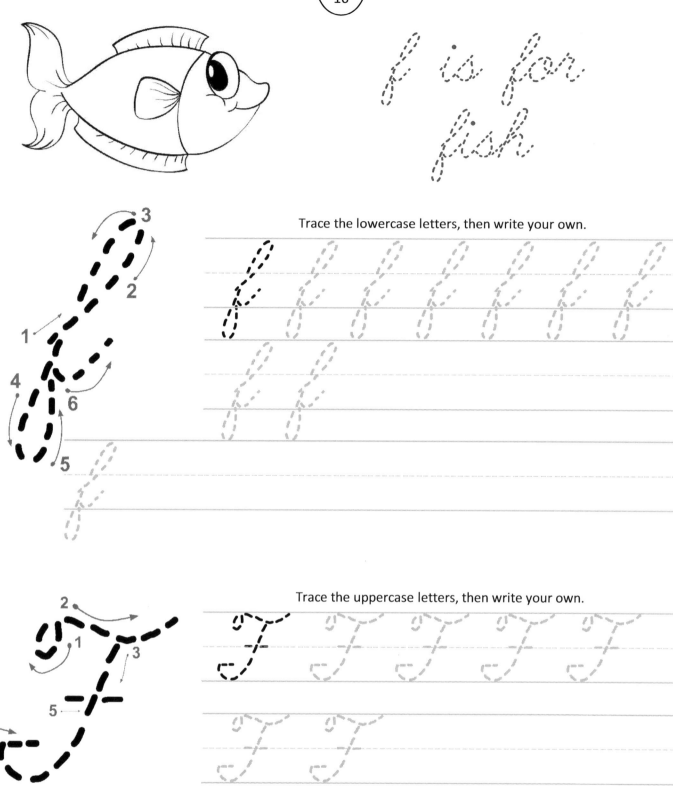

f is for fish

Trace the lowercase letters, then write your own.

Trace the uppercase letters, then write your own.

A B C D E **F** G H I J K L M N O P Q R S T U V W X Y Z

Trace the lowercase letter, then write your own.

Trace the uppercase letter, then write your own.

A B C D E F G H I J K L M N O P Q R S T U V W X Y Z

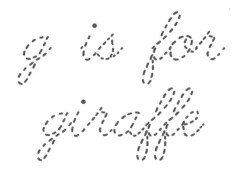

g is for giraffe

Trace the lowercase letters, then write your own.

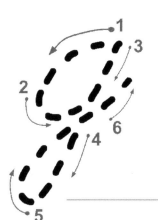

Trace the uppercase letters, then write your own.

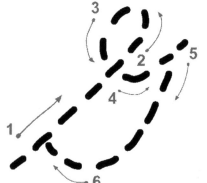

| A | B | C | D | E | F | **G** | H | I | J | K | L | M | N | O | P | Q | R | S | T | U | V | W | X | Y | Z |

Trace the lowercase letter, then write your own.

Trace the uppercase letter, then write your own.

A B C D E F **G** H I J K L M N O P Q R S T U V W X Y Z

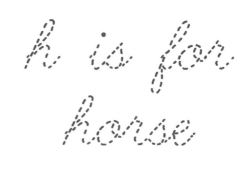

h is for horse

Trace the lowercase letters, then write your own.

Trace the uppercase letters, then write your own.

A B C D E F G **H** I J K L M N O P Q R S T U V W X Y Z

Trace the lowercase letter, then write your own.

Trace the uppercase letter, then write your own.

A B C D E F G H I J K L M N O P Q R S T U V W X Y Z

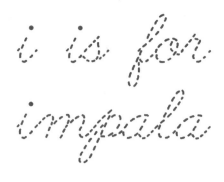

i is for impala

Trace the lowercase letters, then write your own.

Trace the uppercase letters, then write your own.

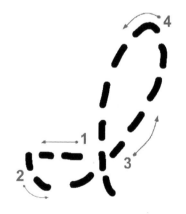

A B C D E F G H I J K L M N O P Q R S T U V W X Y Z

Trace the lowercase letter, then write your own.

Trace the uppercase letter, then write your own.

A B C D E F G H I J K L M N O P Q R S T U V W X Y Z

j is for jaguar

Trace the lowercase letters, then write your own.

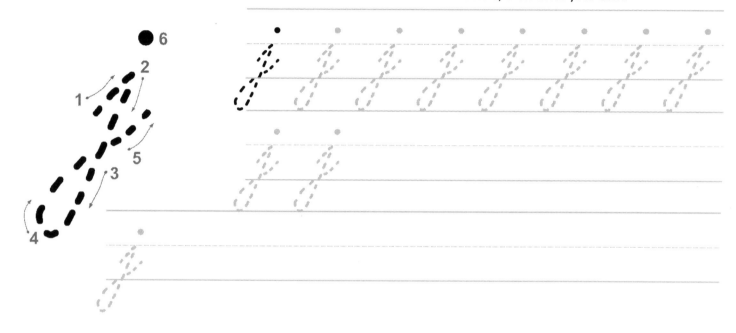

Trace the uppercase letters, then write your own.

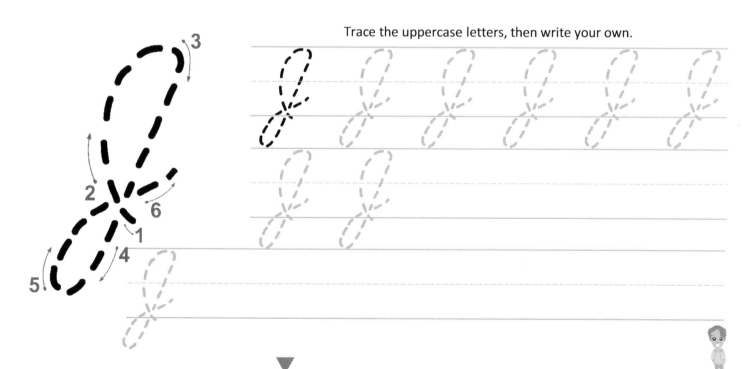

A B C D E F G H I **J** K L M N O P Q R S T U V W X Y Z

Trace the lowercase letter, then write your own.

Trace the uppercase letter, then write your own.

A B C D E F G H I J K L M N O P Q R S T U V W X Y Z

k is for
kangaroo

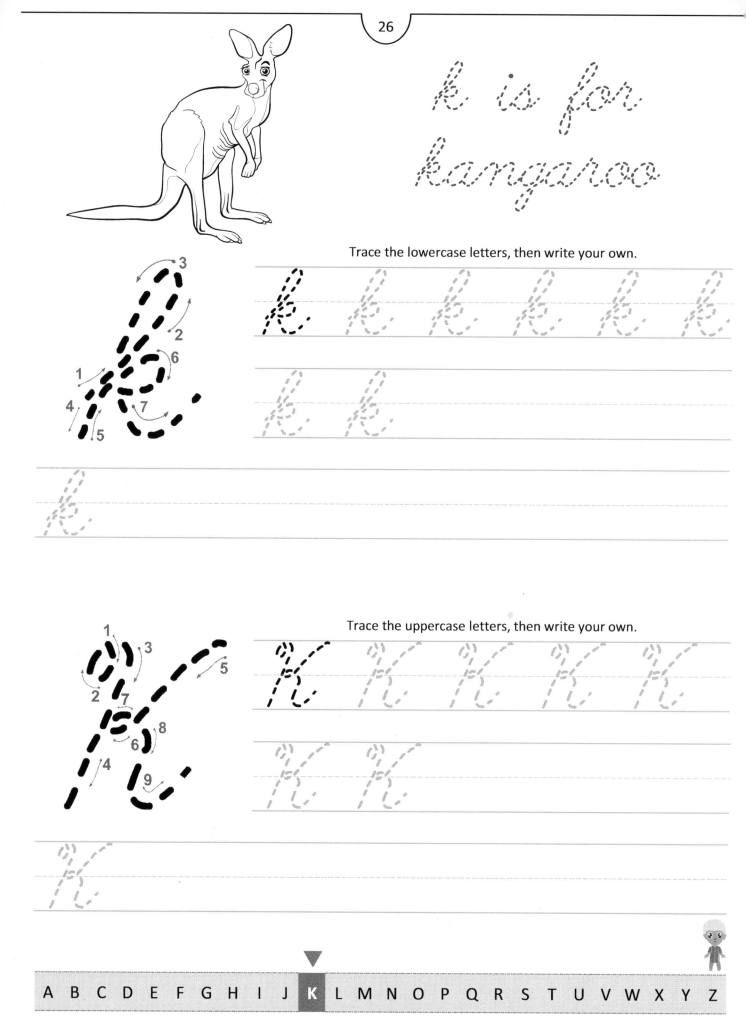

Trace the lowercase letters, then write your own.

Trace the uppercase letters, then write your own.

A B C D E F G H I J **K** L M N O P Q R S T U V W X Y Z

Trace the lowercase letter, then write your own.

Trace the uppercase letter, then write your own.

A B C D E F G H I J K L M N O P Q R S T U V W X Y Z

l is for lion

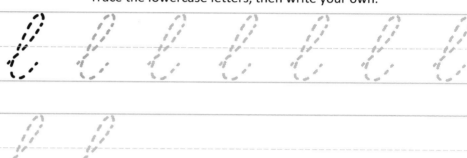

Trace the lowercase letters, then write your own.

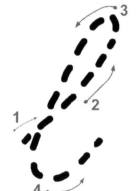

Trace the uppercase letters, then write your own.

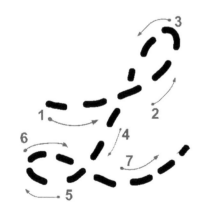

A B C D E F G H I J K **L** M N O P Q R S T U V W X Y Z

Trace the lowercase letter, then write your own.

Trace the uppercase letter, then write your own.

A B C D E F G H I J K L M N O P Q R S T U V W X Y Z

*m is for
monkey*

Trace the lowercase letters, then write your own.

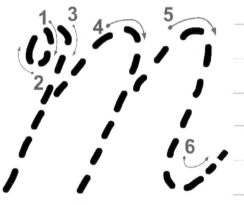

Trace the uppercase letters, then write your own.

A B C D E F G H I J K L **M** N O P Q R S T U V W X Y Z

Trace the lowercase letter, then write your own.

Trace the uppercase letter, then write your own.

A B C D E F G H I J K L **M** N O P Q R S T U V W X Y Z

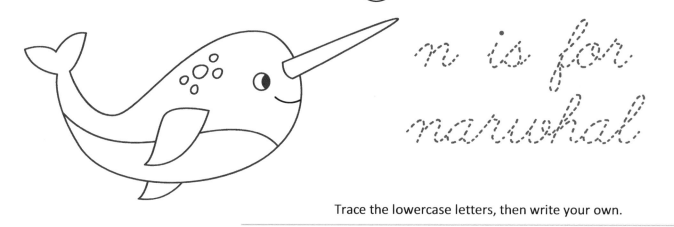

n is for narwhal

Trace the lowercase letters, then write your own.

Trace the uppercase letters, then write your own.

A B C D E F G H I J K L M N O P Q R S T U V W X Y Z

Trace the lowercase letter, then write your own.

Trace the uppercase letter, then write your own.

A B C D E F G H I J K L M N O P Q R S T U V W X Y Z

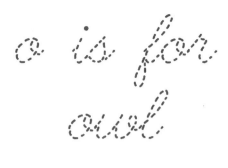

o is for owl

Trace the lowercase letters, then write your own.

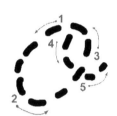

Trace the uppercase letters, then write your own.

A B C D E F G H I J K L M N **O** P Q R S T U V W X Y Z

Trace the lowercase letter, then write your own.

Trace the uppercase letter, then write your own.

A B C D E F G H I J K L M N O P Q R S T U V W X Y Z

p is for penguin

Trace the lowercase letters, then write your own.

Trace the uppercase letters, then write your own.

A B C D E F G H I J K L M N O **P** Q R S T U V W X Y Z

Trace the lowercase letter, then write your own.

Trace the uppercase letter, then write your own.

A B C D E F G H I J K L M N O P Q R S T U V W X Y Z

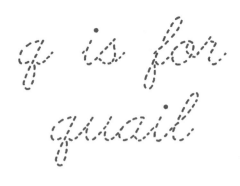

q is for
quail

Trace the lowercase letters, then write your own.

Trace the uppercase letters, then write your own.

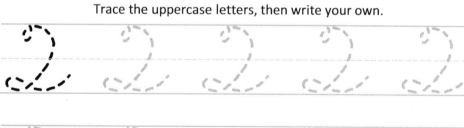

A B C D E F G H I J K L M N O P Q R S T U V W X Y Z

Trace the lowercase letter, then write your own.

Trace the uppercase letter, then write your own.

A B C D E F G H I J K L M N O P Q R S T U V W X Y Z

n is for

raccoon

Trace the lowercase letters, then write your own.

Trace the uppercase letters, then write your own.

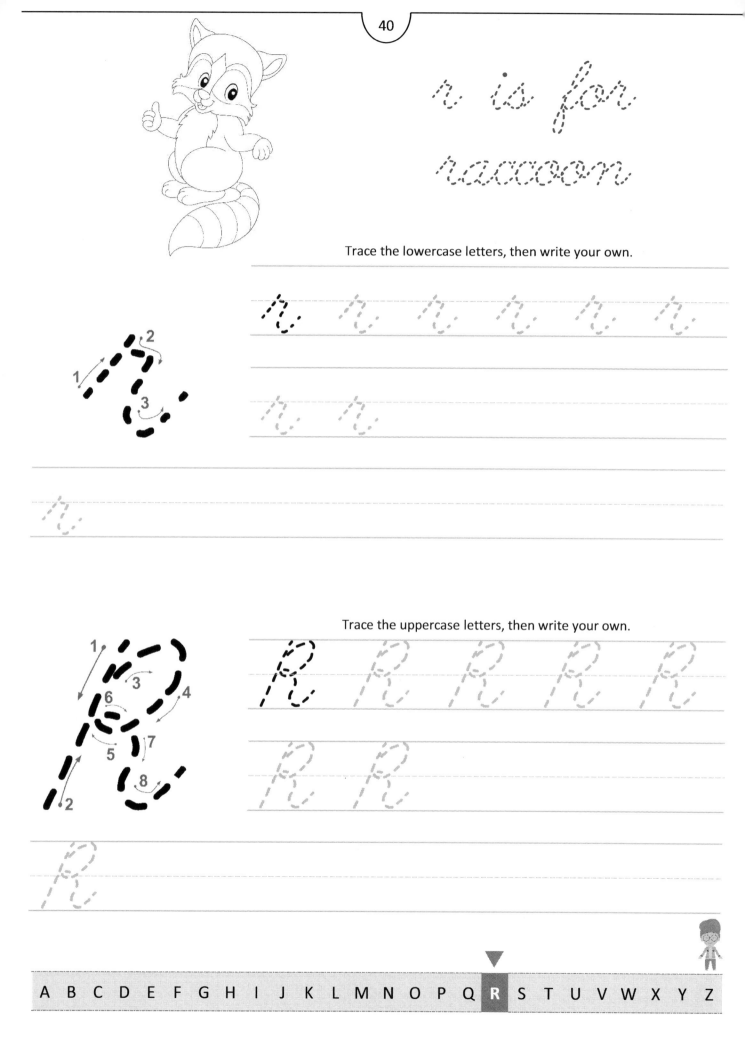

A B C D E F G H I J K L M N O P Q **R** S T U V W X Y Z

Trace the lowercase letter, then write your own.

Trace the uppercase letter, then write your own.

A B C D E F G H I J K L M N O P Q **R** S T U V W X Y Z

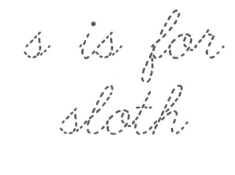

s is for sloth

Trace the lowercase letters, then write your own.

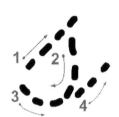

Trace the uppercase letters, then write your own.

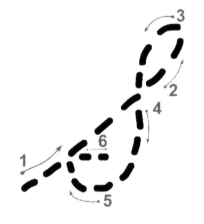

| A | B | C | D | E | F | G | H | I | J | K | L | M | N | O | P | Q | R | **S** | T | U | V | W | X | Y | Z |

Trace the lowercase letter, then write your own.

Trace the uppercase letter, then write your own.

A B C D E F G H I J K L M N O P Q R **S** T U V W X Y Z

t is for turtle

Trace the lowercase letters, then write your own.

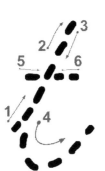

t t t t t t t

t t

t

Trace the uppercase letters, then write your own.

A B C D E F G H I J K L M N O P Q R S **T** U V W X Y Z

Trace the lowercase letter, then write your own.

Trace the uppercase letter, then write your own.

A B C D E F G H I J K L M N O P Q R S T U V W X Y Z

u is for unicorn

Trace the lowercase letters, then write your own.

Trace the uppercase letters, then write your own.

A B C D E F G H I J K L M N O P Q R S T **U** V W X Y Z

Trace the lowercase letter, then write your own.

Trace the uppercase letter, then write your own.

A B C D E F G H I J K L M N O P Q R S T U V W X Y Z

v is for

vulture

Trace the lowercase letters, then write your own.

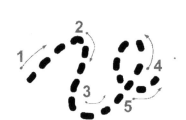

Trace the uppercase letters, then write your own.

| A | B | C | D | E | F | G | H | I | J | K | L | M | N | O | P | Q | R | S | T | U | V | W | X | Y | Z |

Trace the lowercase letter, then write your own.

Trace the uppercase letter, then write your own.

A B C D E F G H I J K L M N O P Q R S T U **V** W X Y Z

w is for

whale

Trace the lowercase letters, then write your own.

Trace the uppercase letters, then write your own.

A B C D E F G H I J K L M N O P Q R S T U V W X Y Z

Trace the lowercase letter, then write your own.

Trace the uppercase letter, then write your own.

A B C D E F G H I J K L M N O P Q R S T U V **W** X Y Z

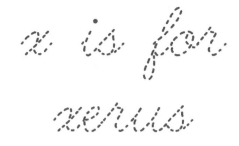

x is for xerus

Trace the lowercase letters, then write your own.

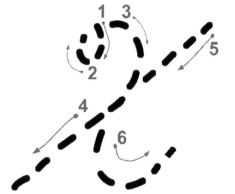

Trace the uppercase letters, then write your own.

A B C D E F G H I J K L M N O P Q R S T U V W **X** Y Z

Trace the lowercase letter, then write your own.

Trace the uppercase letter, then write your own.

A B C D E F G H I J K L M N O P Q R S T U V W X Y Z

Y is for yak

Trace the lowercase letters, then write your own.

Trace the uppercase letters, then write your own.

A B C D E F G H I J K L M N O P Q R S T U V W X **Y** Z

Trace the lowercase letter, then write your own.

Trace the uppercase letter, then write your own.

A B C D E F G H I J K L M N O P Q R S T U V W X Y Z

 z is for zebra

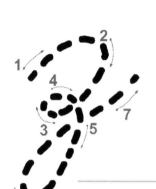

Trace the lowercase letters, then write your own.

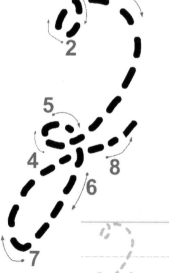

Trace the uppercase letters, then write your own.

A B C D E F G H I J K L M N O P Q R S T U V W X Y Z

Trace the lowercase letter, then write your own.

Trace the uppercase letter, then write your own.

A B C D E F G H I J K L M N O P Q R S T U V W X Y Z

Very good job!

You have now finished Section 1 of your journey towards mastering the art of Cursive Writing.

SECTION 2

WRITING 3-LETTER WORDS

Connecting lowercase cursive letters a-z

Bring together the skills you learnt in Section 1 by writing a selection of words that are composed of 3 letters.

Trace the words, then write your own in the next line.

all all all all all all

and and and and and

age age age age age age

ash ash ash ash ash ash

add add add add add

Trace the words, then write your own in the next line.

big big big big big big big

bee bee bee bee bee bee bee

box box box box box box

boy boy boy boy boy

bye bye bye bye bye bye

A **B** C D E F G H I J K L M N O P Q R S T U V W X Y Z

Trace the words, then write your own in the next line.

can   can   can   can   can   can

cup   cup   cup   cup   cup

cow   cow   cow   cow   cow

cry   cry   cry   cry   cry   cry

can   can   can   can   can

| A | B | C | D | E | F | G | H | I | J | K | L | M | N | O | P | Q | R | S | T | U | V | W | X | Y | Z |

Trace the words, then write your own in the next line.

day day day day day

dog dog dog dog dog dog

dry dry dry dry dry

did did did did did did

due due due due due

A B C **D** E F G H I J K L M N O P Q R S T U V W X Y Z

Trace the words, then write your own in the next line.

eat eat eat eat eat eat

egg egg egg egg egg egg egg

era era era era era era

eye eye eye eye eye eye

end end end end end

A B C D **E** F G H I J K L M N O P Q R S T U V W X Y Z

Trace the words, then write your own in the next line.

far far far far far far

fee fee fee fee fee fee fee

fly fly fly fly fly fly

fix fix fix fix fix fix fix

fun fun fun fun fun

A	B	C	D	E	**F**	G	H	I	J	K	L	M	N	O	P	Q	R	S	T	U	V	W	X	Y	Z

Trace the words, then write your own in the next line.

gas gas gas gas gas gas

gel gel gel gel gel gel gel

guy guy guy guy guy

gym gym gym gym

get get get get get get get

| A | B | C | D | E | F | **G** | H | I | J | K | L | M | N | O | P | Q | R | S | T | U | V | W | X | Y | Z |

Trace the words, then write your own in the next line.

hat hat hat hat hat hat

hug hug hug hug hug

him him him him him

hen hen hen hen hen hen

hue hue hue hue hue hue

A B C D E F G **H** I J K L M N O P Q R S T U V W X Y Z

Trace the words, then write your own in the next line.

ice ice ice ice ice ice ice

ink ink ink ink ink

ill ill ill ill ill ill ill

ion ion ion ion ion ion

ivy ivy ivy ivy ivy

A B C D E F G H **I** J K L M N O P Q R S T U V W X Y Z

Trace the words, then write your own in the next line.

jet jet jet jet jet jet jet

jar jar jar jar jar jar

joy joy joy joy joy joy

jam jam jam jam jam

jut jut jut jut jut jut

| A | B | C | D | E | F | G | H | I | J | K | L | M | N | O | P | Q | R | S | T | U | V | W | X | Y | Z |

Trace the words, then write your own in the next line.

key key key key key

kid kid kid kid kid kid

kit kit kit kit kit kit

keg keg keg keg keg keg

kin kin kin kin kin

A B C D E F G H I J **K** L M N O P Q R S T U V W X Y Z

Trace the words, then write your own in the next line.

law law law law law

leg leg leg leg leg leg leg

lad lad lad lad lad lad

lie lie lie lie lie lie lie

lot lot lot lot lot lot lot

A B C D E F G H I J K **L** M N O P Q R S T U V W X Y Z

Trace the words, then write your own in the next line.

mom mom mom mom

men men men men

mud mud mud mud

max max max max

mug mug mug mug

A B C D E F G H I J K L **M** N O P Q R S T U V W X Y Z

Trace the words, then write your own in the next line.

new new new new

nut nut nut nut nut

new new new new new

nug nug nug nug nug

not not not not not

A B C D E F G H I J K L M **N** O P Q R S T U V W X Y Z

Trace the words, then write your own in the next line.

oat oat oat oat oat oat

odd odd odd odd odd

oak oak oak oak oak oak

one one one one one one

owl owl owl owl owl

A B C D E F G H I J K L M N O P Q R S T U V W X Y Z

Trace the words, then write your own in the next line.

pen pen pen pen pen

pie pie pie pie pie pie pie

pay pay pay pay pay pay

paw paw paw paw paw

pet pet pet pet pet pet

| A | B | C | D | E | F | G | H | I | J | K | L | M | N | O | P | Q | R | S | T | U | V | W | X | Y | Z |

Trace the words, then write your own in the next line.

qua qua qua qua qua

qed qed qed qed qed qed

qum qum qum qum

qod qod qod qod qod qod

qis qis qis qis qis qis

A B C D E F G H I J K L M N O P Q R S T U V W X Y Z

Trace the words, then write your own in the next line.

red red red red red red

run run run run run

rat rat rat rat rat rat

ray ray ray ray ray

have have have have have

A B C D E F G H I J K L M N O P Q **R** S T U V W X Y Z

Trace the words, then write your own in the next line.

sky sky sky sky sky

sea sea sea sea sea sea

sun sun sun sun sun

sty sty sty sty sty sty

shy shy shy shy shy

A B C D E F G H I J K L M N O P Q R **S** T U V W X Y Z

Trace the words, then write your own in the next line.

two two two two two

too too too too too too

try try try try try

toe toe toe toe toe toe toe

tax tax tax tax tax tax

A B C D E F G H I J K L M N O P Q R S **T** U V W X Y Z

Trace the words, then write your own in the next line.

use use use use use use

ufo ufo ufo ufo ufo ufo

usa usa usa usa usa

url url url url url

urn urn urn urn urn

A B C D E F G H I J K L M N O P Q R S T **U** V W X Y Z

Trace the words, then write your own in the next line.

vain   vain   vain   vain   vain

ven   ven   ven   ven   ven   ven

value   value   value   value   value

via   via   via   via   via   via

vat   vat   vat   vat   vat

A B C D E F G H I J K L M N O P Q R S T U **V** W X Y Z

Trace the words, then write your own in the next line.

way way way way

win win win win win

wet wet wet wet wet

why why why why

web web web web web

A B C D E F G H I J K L M N O P Q R S T U V **W** X Y Z

Trace the words, then write your own in the next line.

A B C D E F G H I J K L M N O P Q R S T U V W X Y Z

Trace the words, then write your own in the next line.

you you you you you

yes yes yes yes yes yes

yet yet yet yet yet yet

yews yews yews yews yews

yea yea yea yea yea

A B C D E F G H I J K L M N O P Q R S T U V W X Y Z

Trace the words, then write your own in the next line.

Great performance!

*You have now finished **Section 2** of your journey towards mastering the art of Cursive Writing.*

SECTION 3

WRITING 4-LETTER WORDS

Connecting uppercase cursive letters A-Z

Let's practice a bit more by exploring words composed of 4 letters this time and connecting more letters to uppercase ones.

Trace the words, then write your own in the next line.

Atom Atom Atom

Able Able Able Able

Also Also Also Also

Army Army Army

Away Away Away

A B C D E F G H I J K L M N O P Q R S T U V W X Y Z

Trace the words, then write your own in the next line.

Ball Ball Ball Ball

Base Base Base Base

Bulb Bulb Bulb Bulb

Body Body Body Body

Bird Bird Bird Bird

A **B** C D E F G H I J K L M N O P Q R S T U V W X Y Z

Trace the words, then write your own in the next line.

City City City City City

Care Care Care Care Care

Cook Cook Cook Cook Coo

Club Club Club Club

Chin Chin Chin Chin

A B **C** D E F G H I J K L M N O P Q R S T U V W X Y Z

Trace the words, then write your own in the next line.

Done *Done* *Done* *Done*

Dear *Dear* *Dear* *Dear*

Door *Door* *Door* *Door*

Desk *Desk* *Desk* *Desk*

Diet *Diet* *Diet* *Diet* *Diet*

A B C **D** E F G H I J K L M N O P Q R S T U V W X Y Z

Trace the words, then write your own in the next line.

Ease Ease Ease Ease Ease

Edge Edge Edge Edge Edge

Echo Echo Echo Echo Echo

Else Else Else Else Else

Exit Exit Exit Exit Exit

A B C D **E** F G H I J K L M N O P Q R S T U V W X Y Z

Trace the words, then write your own in the next line.

Fish Fish Fish Fish

Five Five Five Five

Feed Feed Feed Feed

Face Face Face Face Face

Free Free Free Free

A B C D E **F** G H I J K L M N O P Q R S T U V W X Y Z

Trace the words, then write your own in the next line.

Girl Girl Girl Girl Girl

Good Good Good Good

Grow Grow Grow Grow

Goat Goat Goat Goat

Glow Glow Glow Glow

A B C D E F **G** H I J K L M N O P Q R S T U V W X Y Z

Trace the words, then write your own in the next line.

High   High   High   High   High

Home   Home   Home   Home

Hand   Hand   Hand   Hand

Head   Head   Head   Head

Huge   Huge   Huge   Huge

| A | B | C | D | E | F | G | **H** | I | J | K | L | M | N | O | P | Q | R | S | T | U | V | W | X | Y | Z |

Trace the words, then write your own in the next line.

Iron Iron Iron Iron

Isle Isle Isle Isle Isle

Idle Idle Idle Idle

Idea Idea Idea Idea

Item Item Item Item

A B C D E F G H **I** J K L M N O P Q R S T U V W X Y Z

Trace the words, then write your own in the next line.

June June June June

Just Just Just Just

Joke Joke Joke Joke Joke

Jail Jail Jail Jail Jail

Jack Jack Jack Jack

A B C D E F G H I **J** K L M N O P Q R S T U V W X Y Z

Trace the words, then write your own in the next line.

King King King King

Kiss Kiss Kiss Kiss Kiss

Knot Knot Knot Knot

Keep Keep Keep Keep Keep

Knee Knee Knee Knee

A B C D E F G H I J **K** L M N O P Q R S T U V W X Y Z

Trace the words, then write your own in the next line.

Life Life Life Life Life

Love Love Love Love

Luck Luck Luck Luck

Lake Lake Lake Lake

Left Left Left Left Left

A B C D E F G H I J K **L** M N O P Q R S T U V W X Y Z

Trace the words, then write your own in the next line.

Moon Moon Moon

Make Make Make

Milk Milk Milk Milk

Meat Meat Meat Meat

Much Much Much

A B C D E F G H I J K L **M** N O P Q R S T U V W X Y Z

Trace the words, then write your own in the next line.

Near Near Near Near

Next Next Next Next

Nose Nose Nose Nose

Nail Nail Nail Nail

Nine Nine Nine Nine

A B C D E F G H I J K L M N O P Q R S T U V W X Y Z

Trace the words, then write your own in the next line.

Open Open Open Open

Oven Oven Oven Oven

Once Once Once Once

Oath Oath Oath Oath

Odor Odor Odor Odor

A B C D E F G H I J K L M N **O** P Q R S T U V W X Y Z

Trace the words, then write your own in the next line.

Play Play Play Play

Push Push Push Push

Palm Palm Palm Palm

Pole Pole Pole Pole Pole

Prey Prey Prey Prey

A B C D E F G H I J K L M N O **P** Q R S T U V W X Y Z

Trace the words, then write your own in the next line.

Quad Quad Quad Quad

Quay Quay Quay

Quig Quig Quig Quig

Quit Quit Quit Quit

Quid Quid Quid Quid

A B C D E F G H I J K L M N O P Q R S T U V W X Y Z

Trace the words, then write your own in the next line.

Rain Rain Rain Rain

Rich Rich Rich Rich Rich

Roof Roof Roof Roof Roof

Rust Rust Rust Rust

Read Read Read Read

A B C D E F G H I J K L M N O P Q **R** S T U V W X Y Z

Trace the words, then write your own in the next line.

Safe Safe Safe Safe Safe

Star Star Star Star

Sing Sing Sing Sing

Sure Sure Sure Sure

Skin Skin Skin Skin

A B C D E F G H I J K L M N O P Q R S T U V W X Y Z

Trace the words, then write your own in the next line.

Time Time Time Time

True True True True

Talk Talk Talk Talk

Thin Thin Thin Thin

Tube Tube Tube Tube

A B C D E F G H I J K L M N O P Q R S **T** U V W X Y Z

Trace the words, then write your own in the next line.

User User User User

Ugly Ugly Ugly Ugly

Upon Upon Upon Upon

Urge Urge Urge Urge

Unto Unto Unto Unto

A B C D E F G H I J K L M N O P Q R S T **U** V W X Y Z

Trace the words, then write your own in the next line.

Vase Vase Vase Vase

Vein Vein Vein Vein

Very Very Very Very

Void Void Void Void

View View View View

A B C D E F G H I J K L M N O P Q R S T U **V** W X Y Z

Trace the words, then write your own in the next line.

Wise Wise Wise Wise

Word Word Word

What What What

Well Well Well Well

Wife Wife Wife Wife

A B C D E F G H I J K L M N O P Q R S T U V **W** X Y Z

Trace the words, then write your own in the next line.

Xmas Xmas Xmas

Xian Xian Xian Xian

Xyst Xyst Xyst Xyst

Xien Xien Xien Xien

Xade Xade Xade Xade

A B C D E F G H I J K L M N O P Q R S T U V W **X** Y Z

Trace the words, then write your own in the next line.

Yeah. Yeah. Yeah. Yeah.

Yard Yard Yard Yard

Year. Year. Year. Year.

Yell Yell Yell Yell Yell

Yore Yore Yore Yore

A B C D E F G H I J K L M N O P Q R S T U V W X **Y** Z

Trace the words, then write your own in the next line.

Zoom Zoom Zoom Zoom

Zone Zone Zone Zone

Zina Zina Zina Zina

Zero Zero Zero Zero Zero

Zest Zest Zest Zest Zest

Excellent work!

*You have now finished **Section 3** of your journey towards mastering the art of Cursive Writing.*

SECTION 4

WRITING FREQUENT WORDS

...with variable number of letters!

Now let's move on to writing more complex words, with varying number of letters.

Trace the words, then write your own in the same line and in the next.

Actor actor actor.

Agree agree agree

Above above above

Across across across

Alert alert alert

Among among among

Trace the words, then write your own in the same line and in the next.

angry angry

annoy annoy annoy

another another another

award award award

aware aware aware

badge badge badge

Trace the words, then write your own in the same line and in the next.

Basic basic basic

Battle battle battle

Beast beast beast

Board board board

Build build build

Burst burst burst

Trace the words, then write your own in the same line and in the next.

cactus Cactus Cactus

careless careless careless

chase chase chase

chimney chimney chimney

circus circus circus

close close close

Trace the words, then write your own in the same line and in the next.

Clothing clothing clothing

Coach coach coach

Coming coming coming

Crawl crawl crawl

Deaf deaf deaf

Double double double

Trace the words, then write your own in the same line and in the next.

equal equal equal

evening evening evening

everything everything

flour flour flour

flower flower flower

froge froge froge

Trace the words, then write your own in the same line and in the next.

Garbage garbage

Growl growl growl

Hollow hollow hollow

Honey honey honey

Hoping hoping hoping

Include include include

Trace the words, then write your own in the same line and in the next.

insist insist insist

jeans jeans jeans

kitchen kitchen kitchen

lace lace lace

laugh laugh laugh

little little little

Trace the words, then write your own in the same line and in the next.

Marble marble

Match match match

Midnight midnight

Monkey monkey

Newspaper newspaper

Offer offer offer

Trace the words, then write your own in the same line and in the next.

Pillow pillow

Porch porch porch

Recover recover

Remember remember

Report report report

Riddle riddle riddle

Trace the words, then write your own in the same line and in the next.

scale scale scale

scrape scrape scrape

scream scream

seashore seashore

season season season

shallow shallow

Trace the words, then write your own in the same line and in the next.

shrimp shrimp

sidewalk sidewalk

simple simple

slate slate slate

sleeve sleeve sleeve

stepped stepped

Trace the words, then write your own in the same line and in the next.

Stopped stopped

Strong strong

Thrill thrill thrill

Ticket ticket ticket

Title title title

Torch torch torch

Trace the words, then write your own in the same line and in the next.

Trace trace trace

Unlock unlock

Visitor visitor

Value value value

Wonder wonder

White write write

Fantastic!

You have now finished **Section 4** of your journey towards mastering the art of Cursive Writing.

SECTION 5

WRITING SHORT SENTENCES

Connecting words to form entire sentence

It's time for more fun. Let's practice writing full sentences by copying the short stories provided in this section.

Trace the sentence, then write your own in the next line.

Beach Ball

Oliver has a beach ball

the beach ball is big

he plays with his friends

what color is the ball?

Oliver has so much fun playing

Trace the sentence, then write your own in the next line.

Picnic

My family went to a picnic

We took a picnic basket

We had sandwiches and chips

Then we went to play

The ants found our food

Trace the sentence, then write your own in the next line.

Watermelon

James likes watermelon

he eats it in the summer

he shares with his friends

they ate it all up

did you want some?

Trace the sentence, then write your own in the next line.

Cupcakes

Mom baked cupcakes

I ate two cupcakes

I shared with my friends

Will mom make more?

They were yummy.

Trace the sentence, then write your own in the next line.

The Zoo

Ben is going to the zoo

Ben wants to see the lion

dad takes Ben to see the lion

Ben saw a monkey at the zoo

Ben saw a hippo at the zoo

Trace the sentence, then write your own in the next line.

The Night Bat

The bat's name is batty

batty likes to fly

e flies at night

e looks for bugs

an you see batty up in the sky?

Trace the sentence, then write your own in the next line.

Penguins

I see five penguins

they are black and white

fish is their favorite food

they are on the ice

sliding is fun.

Trace the sentence, then write your own in the next line.

I like fish.

Ben is at the pond.

He likes to fish.

Ben got a big fish.

His father will cook the fish.

The fish are delicious and healthy.

Trace the sentence, then write your own in the next line.

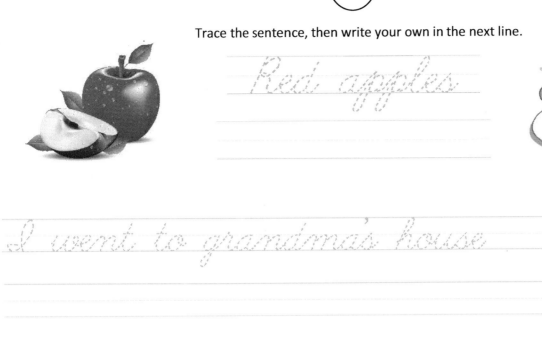

Red apples

I went to grandma's house

we picked red apples

grandma made apple pie for us

they were yummy

it was fun picking apples.

Trace the sentence, then write your own in the next line.

Sunglasses

Peter has red sunglasses

He wears them outside

They protect his eyes

Do you like his sunglasses?

Peter's sunglasses are cool.

Trace the sentence, then write your own in the next line.

Doctor

This is Alex

Alex is a doctor

a doctor works at the hospital

doctors have an important job

doctors help us if we are sick.

Trace the sentence, then write your own in the next line.

Sports

We love sports.

We like to play football.

We like to play soccer.

We play sports every Friday.

What sports do you like to play?

Trace the sentence, then write your own in the next line.

I like gum!

Yum! I like gum!

I like to chew gum

I like to chew gum and bum

my mum has gum, she gives me som

yum! yum! I like to chew gum!

Trace the sentence, then write your own in the next line.

Spot can trot.

Spot is a horse

Spot can run, can run fast

Spot can trot, can trot fast

Spot wins a lot

e is a hot shot!

Trace the sentence, then write your own in the next line.

Cat has a hat

Nat has a big cat

the cat has a big hat

the cat is on a mat, it is a big mat

Nat likes the hat, Nat likes the mat

Nat likes the big cat.

Trace the sentence, then write your own in the next line.

Pam has jam

Pam has a bit of jam

The jam is not in a bag

The jam is not in a pan

The jam is in a can

The jam is not bad

Trace the sentence, then write your own in the next line.

My friend

Fred is my friend

Fred is from Texas

Fred has a lot of freckles

Fred also has a pet frog

Fred's favorite food is french fries

Trace the sentence, then write your own in the next line.

Spicy Rice

I make a pot of rice. It is spicy!

t has hot sauce in it

my face gets red. That rice is hot!

I take a sip of iced tea, then

I have more rice. I love spicy rice!

You are exceptional!

*You have now finished **Section 5** of your journey towards mastering the art of Cursive Writing.*

SECTION 6

WRITING MONTHS & DAYS

Now, you are mastering cursive writing!

You have made it — one section is left. Bring together all the skills you learnt in previous sections and write the most beautiful months and days names, and compare it with your initial cursive writing...

What a huge progress!!

Trace the word, then write your own in the same line and continue in the next.

Monday

Tuesday

Wednesday

Thursday

Friday

Saturday

Sunday

Trace the word, then write your own in the same line and continue in the next.

January

February

March

April

May

June

Trace the word, then write your own in the same line and continue in the next.

July

August

September

October

November

December

Outstanding!

You have finished Section 6!

You are now mastering the art of Cursive Writing.

DIPLOMA

THIS CERTIFICATE IS PRESENTED TO

_____

BY *Andrea Holden*
_____

For mastering the art of Cursive Writing in such a fast and brilliant way!

DATE _____

SIGNATURE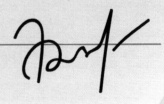

Printed in Great Britain
by Amazon